Schochler Primary School

_____of_____

THE NEW FOOD GUIDE PYRAMID

Oils

by Emily K. Green

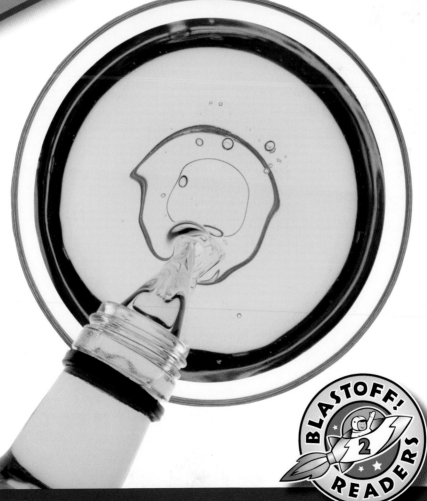

BELLWETHER MEDIA · MINNEAPOLIS, MN

BLASTOFF!
2
READERS

Note to Librarians, Teachers, and Parents:

Blastoff! Readers are carefully developed by literacy experts and combine standards-based content with developmentally appropriate text.

Level 1 provides the most support through repetition of high-frequency words, light text, predictable sentence patterns, and strong visual support.

Level 2 offers early readers a bit more challenge through varied simple sentences, increased text load, and less repetition of high-frequency words.

Level 3 advances early-fluent readers toward fluency through increased text and concept load, less reliance on visuals, longer sentences, and more literary language.

Whichever book is right for your reader, Blastoff! Readers are the perfect books to build confidence and encourage a love of reading that will last a lifetime!

This edition first published in 2007 by Bellwether Media.

No part of this publication may be reproduced in whole or in part without written permission of the publisher. For information regarding permission, write to Bellwether Media Inc., Attention: Permissions Department, Post Office Box 1C, Minnetonka, MN 55345-9998.

Library of Congress Cataloging-in-Publication Data
Green, Emily K., 1966–
  Oils / by Emily K. Green.
     p. cm. – (Blastoff! readers) (New food guide pyramid)
  Includes bibliographical references and index.
Summary: "A basic introduction to the health benefits of oils. Intended for kindergarten through third grade students."
  ISBN-10: 1-60014-001-7 (hardcover : alk. paper)
  ISBN-13: 978-1-60014-001-3 (hardcover : alk. paper)
  1. Vegetable oils in human nutrition—Juvenile literature. 2. Lipids in human nutrition—Juvenile literature. 3. Nutrition—Juvenile literature. I. Title. II. Series.

  QP144.O44G74 2007
  613.2–dc22   2006000405

Table of Contents

The **food guide pyramid** helps kids choose healthy foods.

The Food Guide Pyramid

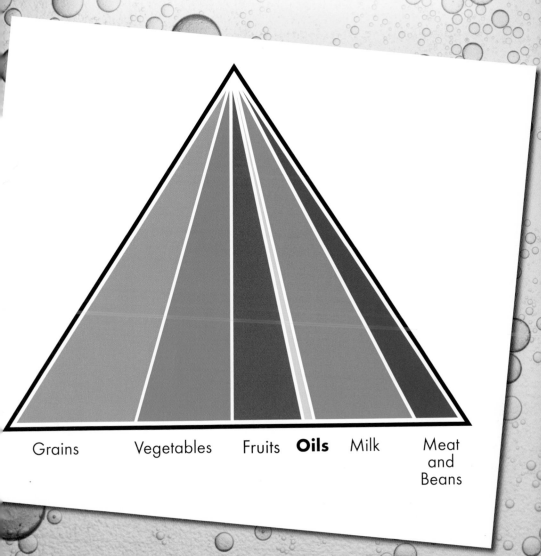

Grains   Vegetables   Fruits   **Oils**   Milk   Meat and Beans

Each color stripe on the pyramid stands for a food group. The yellow stripe is oils.

Oils are **liquid fats** that are healthy for you.

Corn, olive, and sunflower oils are fats that are healthy for you.

Fat in oils helps carry **vitamins** through your body. Fat in oils gives you **energy**.

8

Fat in oils helps your brain work well.

It is important to have some oils in your food every day.

But don't eat more than you need.

5

Kids need about five teaspoons of oils a day.

You can get all the liquid
fats you need just by eating
healthy foods.

Solid fats are not as
healthy for you.

Butter is a solid fat.

Eating too much fat is
not good for you.

Fried foods have a lot of fat.
It's best not to eat too much
fried food.

Most desserts have a
lot of fat.

It is best to save desserts for special times.

How Much Should A Kid Eat Each Day?

Vegetables
2½ cups

Oils
5 teaspoons

Grains
6 servings

Fruits
1 ½ cups

Milk, Yogurt, and Cheese
3 cups

Meat and Beans
1-2 servings

Glossary

energy—the power to move

fat—a part of some foods that gives you energy and helps your body use vitamins

fried—cooked in hot oil

food guide pyramid—a chart showing the kinds and amounts of foods you should eat each day

liquid—something that is not solid nor frozen; liquids take the shape of their surroundings.

solid—something that is not liquid. Butter is solid fat.

vitamins—parts of some foods that keep your body healthy; vitamin C helps you heal from cuts and colds.

To Learn More

AT THE LIBRARY

Barron, Rex. *Showdown at the Food Pyramid.* Putnam, 2004.

Leedy, Loreen. *The Edible Pyramid: Good Eating Every Day.* New York: Holiday House, 1994.

Rabe, Tish. *Oh The Things You Can Do That Are Good For You: All About Staying Healthy.* New York: Random House, 2001.

Rockwell, Lizzy. *Good Enough to Eat: A Kid's Guide to Food And Nutrition.* New York: HarperCollins, 1999.

ON THE WEB

Learning more about healthy eating is as easy as 1, 2, 3.

1. Go to www.factsurfer.com

2. Enter "healthy eating" into search box.

3. Click the "Surf" button and you will see a list of related web sites.

With factsurfer.com, finding more information is just a click away.

Index

The photographs in this book are reproduced through the courtesy of: David Seed Photography/Getty Images, front cover; Mike Powell/Getty Images, p. 4; Aaron Graubart/Getty Images, p. 5; Jonelle Weaver/Getty Images, p. 6; Johnnny Lye, p. 7(top); luminouslens, p. 7(middle); Susi Bikle, p. 7(bottom); Steve Lewis/Getty Images, p. 8; Photo Create, p. 9; Michael Rosenfeld/Getty Images, pp. 10-11; Dorling Kindersley/Getty Images, p. 12; Magdalena Kucova, p. 13; GSO Images/Getty Images, pp. 14-15; Dragan Trifunovic, p. 16; Liv friss-larsen, p. 17; Susi Bikle, p. 18; Edyta Linek, p. 19; Juan Martinez, p. 20(top); Michael Rosenfeld/Getty Images, p.20(middle); Tim McClellan, p. 20(bottom), p. 21(top,bottom); Olga Lyubkina, p. 21(middle).

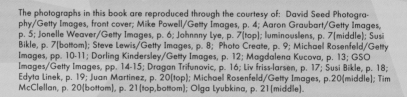